THE CONTINENT OF EUROPE

The land areas of the world are divided into seven co
North America, **South America**, **Europe**, **Africa**, **Asia**, and **Antarctica**.

Each continent is made up of a number of different countries. In Europe there are over thirty.

Which continent do you live in?

In northern Europe it is cold and icy in winter and warm in summer.
Countries in southern Europe have long, hot, dry summers and mild winters.
Which sort of weather do you prefer?

Read about the different foods, languages, costumes, money and traditions.

See how many differences and similarities there are between your country and other countries in Europe.

There are puzzles and quizzes, too. Have fun!

THE EUROPEAN COMMUNITY

The 12 countries shaded in yellow on the map are all members of the *European Community (EC)*.

The aim of the EC is to help the countries who belong to the Community to work and trade together more easily.

How the EC began

1951 Belgium, France, Germany, Italy, Luxembourg, and the Netherlands agree to link their coal, iron and steel industries. Their agreement is known as the Treaty of Paris

1952 The European Coal and Steel Community is formed

1957 The same countries sign the Treaty of Rome to create the European Economic Community (EEC)

1973 Denmark, Ireland and the UK join the EEC

1981 Greece joins the Community

1986 Portugal and Spain join the Community

1987 – 1990's Other countries in Europe eager to join the EC include Austria, Cyprus, Malta, Sweden and Turkey

1991 European Free Trade Association (Efta) – Austria, Switzerland, Finland, Iceland and Liechtenstein – link with the EC

1992 Single European Market. Special laws make it easier to work and trade with other countries in the EC

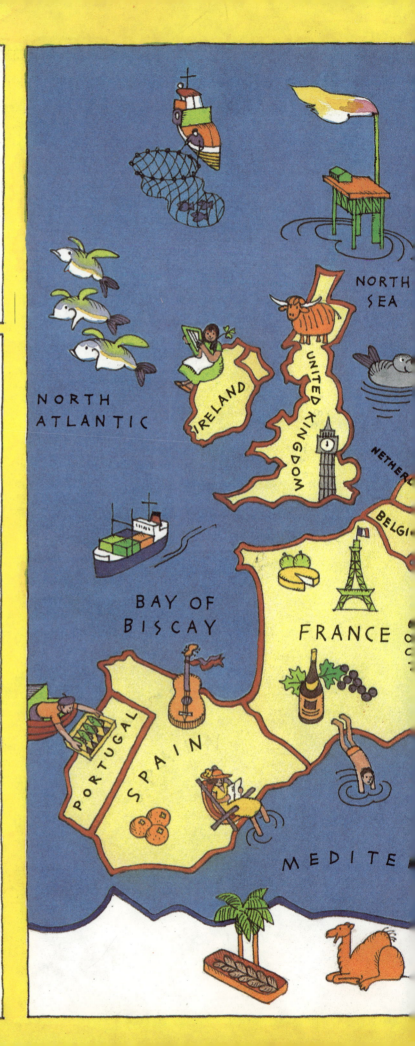

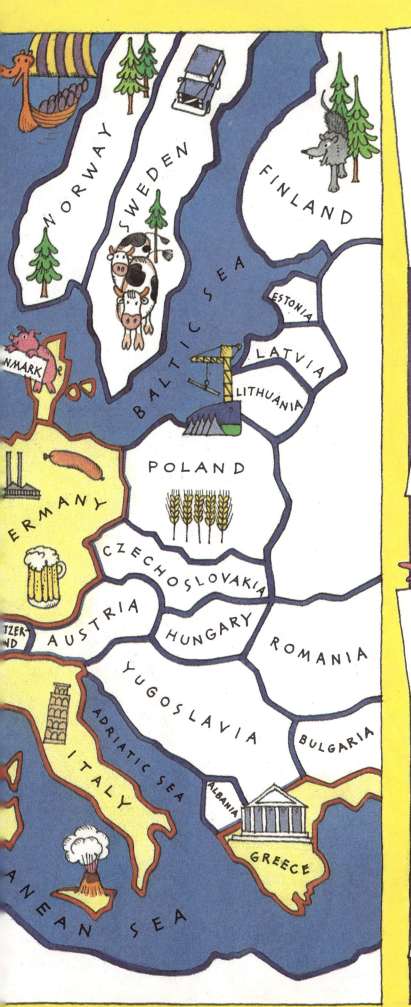

Community flag
This is the EC flag. Each star represents one of the 12 EC countries.

Passports
All European countries used to have their own passports. Now there is a new red European passport for everyone living in the EC.

Money
It is hoped that one day all the EC countries will use the same money – the *European Currency Unit* (ECU). This will make trade between countries much easier and people will not have to change their money when they go abroad on holiday.

One language
In the 1880's Ludovic Zamenhof invented Esperanto, which he hoped would become the international language of Europe. It has a very simple grammar that can be learnt in a couple of hours!

EC FACTFILE

BELGIUM
People Belgian
Population 10 million
Size 33,000 sq km
Capital city Brussels
Languages Flemish, French, German
Money Belgian franc

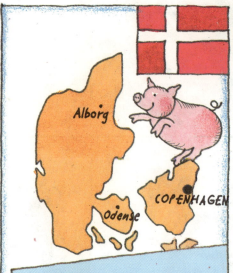

DENMARK
People Danish
Population 5 million
Size 43,000 sq km
Capital city Copenhagen
Language Danish
Money Krone

FRANCE
People French
Population 56 million
Size 547,000 sq km
Capital city Paris
Language French
Money French franc

ITALY
People Italian
Population 57 million
Size 301,000 sq km
Capital city Rome
Language Italian
Money Lira

LUXEMBOURG
People Luxembourger
Population 400 thousand
Size 2,600 sq km
Capital city Luxembourg
Languages French, German, Luxembourgeois
Money Luxembourg franc

NETHERLANDS
People Dutch
Population 15 million
Size 37,000 sq km
Capital city Amsterdam
Language Dutch
Money Guilder

GERMANY

People German
Population 78 million
Size 357,000 sq km
Capital city Berlin
Language German
Money Deutschmark

GREECE

People Greek
Population 10 million
Size 132,000 sq km
Capital city Athens
Language Greek
Money Drachma

IRELAND

People Irish
Population 3.5 million
Size 70,000 sq km
Capital city Dublin
Languages English, Irish
Money Irish pound (punt)

PORTUGAL

People Portuguese
Population 10 million
Size 92,000 sq km
Capital city Lisbon
Language Portuguese
Money Escudo

SPAIN

People Spanish
Population 39 million
Size 505,000 sq km
Capital city Madrid
Language Spanish
Money Peseta

UNITED KINGDOM

People British
Population 57 million
Size 245,000 sq km
Capital city London
Languages English, Welsh
Money Pound

COUNTRY CONNECTIONS

Each of these things is connected with a European country. The first one has been done for you. Can you work out the other connections?

Answers Austria = 11; Belgium = 12; Denmark = 10; France = 5; Germany = 4; Greece = 6; Italy = 1; Netherlands = 3; Norway = 7; Portugal = 9; Spain = 8; Switzerland = 2

NAMES ON STAMPS

Here are some stamps from different countries. Match each stamp to the correct country. Can you spot the odd ones out? ☐ ☐

- ☐ ITALY
- ☐ BELGIUM
- ☐ DENMARK
- ☐ PORTUGAL
- ☐ NETHERLANDS
- ☐ LUXEMBOURG
- ☐ FRANCE
- ☐ CZECHOSLOVAKIA

Look carefully at how the names are spelt on the stamps.

DID YOU KNOW?

* The first adhesive postage stamp was the Penny Black issued in the UK in 1840.
* The UK is the only country in the world that does not have its name on its stamps.
* Liechtenstein, a tiny country on the borders of Austria and Switzerland, issues new stamps every three months – more often than any other country in the world.

Some European stamps

Sometimes it's not so easy to tell where a stamp comes from.
Here are the names written on some European stamps.
Would you have guessed these?

NAME	COUNTRY
Eire	Ireland
España	Spain
Hellas	Greece
Helvetia	Switzerland
Magyar Posta	Hungary
Norge	Norway
Österreich	Austria
Polska	Poland
Sverige	Sweden
Deutsche Bundespost	Germany

Start a stamp collection

All you need is an album (a scrapbook will do) to stick them in.

If you want to keep your stamps in good condition, stick them in the album with stamp hinges (you can buy these from a stationery shop).

Have a separate page for each country. You could even draw a map of the country on the page to make it look more attractive.

Write to a penfriend

A penfriend is someone you can write to and tell about your hobbies and your family, and the things you have done.

If you have a penfriend in a different country, you can get to know about the country they live in, swap stories and photographs and perhaps, if you're lucky, you can go and stay with them for holidays.

Ask your family and friends to save their stamps for you.

If you get two stamps the same, swap with a friend.

If you would like a penfriend write to:

**International Youth Service,
P.O. Box 125,
SF – 20101 Turku,
Finland**

FAMOUS LANDMARKS

Can you name these famous landmarks?
In which country would you find each one?

Eiffel Tower

This tower was built for the 1889 Paris Exhibition, in France, by the French engineer Alexandre-Gustave Eiffel.

It took two years, two months and two days to build, and is made up of over eighteen thousand wrought iron struts joined together by two and a half million nuts and bolts!

It stands 300 m high and sways in strong winds!

Colosseum

The Colosseum in Rome, Italy was built almost two thousand years ago.

It was used as a stadium for holding chariot races and contests between trained fighters called *gladiators*.

The building had 72 stairways leading to 50,000 marble seats for spectators.

Big Ben

This is the name of the big bell that strikes the hour in the clock tower next to the Houses of Parliament in London, England. It is named after Sir Benjamin Hall who was Commissioner for Works when the bell was first used.

People often call the clock tower Big Ben but its correct name is Saint Stephen's Tower.

Acropolis

An acropolis is an ancient fortress built on the top of a hill.

The most famous one was built in 5BC and overlooks the city of Athens, in Greece.

Although much of the building is now in ruins, the Parthenon, a temple to the goddess Athena, still stands.

Leaning Tower

This tower was built at Pisa, in Italy between 1174 and 1350. It leans because it was built on soft sand and mud. It began to lean even while it was being built! The builders tried to correct the lean by altering the length of the pillars on one side but this didn't work.

It's now famous throughout the world as the Leaning Tower of Pisa.

Atomium

This strange, 102 m high steel structure was built in 1958 in Brussels, the capital of Belgium.

It takes the shape of a molecule (a tiny particle) of iron crystal that has been magnified 165 billion times! The nine metal globes are linked together with 3 m wide tunnels that carry stairs and escalators. Inside the globes there are exhibitions on science and technology.

LET'S EAT

Many countries are well known for a special meal. You might have eaten some of these meals or seen them on menus. But do you know in which country you are most likely to see them?

DID YOU KNOW?

* In Gerona, Spain on 25th August, 1987 Josep Gruges cooked the world's biggest paella. When cooked it was 16 m across and it took 40,000 people to eat it!

* There are about 450 different cheeses in the world. Over half of them are made in France.

* The longest sausage in the world was made by a butcher near Wolverhampton, in England. It measured 21.12 km (over 13 miles) long!

Answers Smorrebrod = Denmark; Roast Beef and Yorkshire Pudding = England; Spaghetti Bolognaise = Italy; Dolmades (stuffed vine leaves) = Greece; Goulash = Hungary; Wurst and Sauerkraut (spicy sausage and pickled cabbage) = Germany; Paella = Spain

PIZZA QUATTRO STAGIONI (Four Seasons Pizza)

Here's an Italian recipe to try.
For a pizza big enough for 2/3 people you will need:

for the base
200 g self-raising flour
25 g margarine
150 ml warm water
1 teaspoon salt

for the toppings
olive oil
1 large tomato (sliced)
50 g mozzarella cheese (sliced)
50 g mushrooms (sliced)
50 g chopped ham
50 g chopped salami
black pepper

1 Preheat the oven to 230°C/450°F/Gas mark 8

2 Sieve the flour and the salt into a bowl

3 Cut the margarine into small pieces and use your fingers to mix them into the flour until the mixture feels like breadcrumbs

4 Pour in the water and use a spatula to mix it into the flour to make a dough

5 Bring the dough to a ball with your hands

6 Put it on a flour-covered work surface

7 Use a rolling pin to flatten the dough into a round shape

8 Place the round dough shape onto a greased baking tray

9 Heat about 2 tablespoons of oil in a frying pan

10 Gently fry the mushrooms in the oil for a few minutes

11 Mark the top of the dough into 4 equal sections and brush over with olive oil

12 Add cheese, then different toppings to each quarter

13 Sprinkle some black pepper and a few drops of olive oil over the top of the pizza

14 Bake in a preheated oven for 15 minutes

15 Reduce the oven temperature to 190°C/375°F/Gas mark 5 and bake for a further 10 minutes

16 Eat the pizza!

Experiment with different toppings.

Make a Pizza face.

RIVERS AND MOUNTAINS

The map on these pages shows some of the rivers and mountain ranges in Europe. Use the information on the map opposite to fill in the missing names opposite.

1 It flows through Paris in France _____
2 This river in Ireland is the longest river in the British Isles _____
3 The highest mountain in this range is Mont Blanc _____
4 This river flows through Lisbon, the capital of Portugal _____
5 This beautiful river is a popular tourist attraction for visitors to Germany _____
6 The city of London stands on this famous river _____
7 This is the highest and largest group of mountains in Scotland _____
8 There is a famous waltz named after this river _____
9 These mountains are sometimes called 'the backbone of Italy' _____
10 The capital of Italy is on this river _____
11 This range of mountains separates France and Spain _____
12 This is the highest mountain in Europe _____

Eurofacts

Highest mountains Elbrus (Ukraine) 5,642 m; Mont Blanc (on the borders of France and Italy) 4,807 m
Longest rivers Volga 3,690 km (2,293 miles) flows from the hills north of Moscow to the Caspian Sea*; Danube 2,850 km (1,770 miles) flows from southern Germany to the Black Sea

*Not all of the river Volga is shown on the map. Look it up in an atlas. See if you can trace its journey to the Caspian Sea

CARS AND THEIR COUNTRIES

You can tell which country a motor vehicle comes from by the identification sticker on the back of it. These stickers usually show the first letter of the country's name.

Can you guess which European countries these cars come from?

Would you have guessed these? Some are not so easy!

- (BG) = Bulgaria
- (CH) = Switzerland
- (CS) = Czechoslovakia
- (D) = Germany
- (E) = Spain
- (FL) = Liechtenstein
- (H) = Hungary
- (IRL) = Ireland
- (L) = Luxembourg
- (N) = Norway
- (PL) = Poland
- (RO) = Romania
- (SF) = Finland
- (YU) = Yugoslavia

DID YOU KNOW?

* In the village of Ripatransone, in Italy there is a street which is only 43 cm wide!

* On 16th February, 1980 there was a traffic jam in France 176 km (109 miles) long on the road from Lyon to Paris.

Answers P = Portugal; GB = UK (Great Britain); B = Belgium; A = Austria; F = France; I = Italy; S = Sweden; NL = Netherlands; DK = Denmark; GR = Greece

MONEY, MONEY, MONEY

Each country has its own money or *currency*. The chart below shows some of the currencies from different European countries.

Fill in the gaps to complete the chart.

Country	Currency
Austria	Schilling
Belgium	....
Bulgaria	Lev
Czechoslovakia	Koruna
Denmark	....
France	....
Finland	Markka
Germany	....
....	Drachma
Hungary	Forint
....	Punt
Italy	....
Netherlands	....
Norway	Krone
Poland	Zloty
Portugal	....
....	Peseta
Sweden	Krona
United Kingdom	....

Look back at pages 4 and 5, if you need some help.

Collect some coins

If you ever go abroad on holiday keep some of the coins. Ask your friends to get you some when they go away. Before long you will have an interesting collection. See how many coins you can get from all over Europe.

DID YOU KNOW?

* The ancient Romans, who came from Italy, paid their soldiers with salt. It is from their word for salt that we get our word 'salary' (wages).

* A few years ago there was a shortage of small coins in Portugal so the people used sweets and stamps as money.

COLOURFUL COSTUMES

These dolls are all wearing traditional costumes from Europe. Can you match each doll with its partner to find the six pairs?

Collecting costume dolls

Lots of people collect costume dolls. They bring them back as souvenirs from holiday, or ask friends to bring them back when they go away.

Why not start your own collection?

CELEBRATIONS AND TRADITIONS

Festivals and unusual customs and traditions can be seen in every European country. Here are just a few examples.

Floats and flowers

Two of the most famous festivals of flowers take place in Jersey, in the Channel Islands, and at Nice, in France. Flower covered floats travel through the streets, and the procession ends with a spectacular battle where everyone throws flowers at one another!

Festivals of fire

Every January a group of people from Lerwick, in the Shetland Isles of Scotland, dress up as Vikings. They have a torchlight procession through the town to burn a replica Viking ship, commemorating the Viking raids on the Scottish Isles over a thousand years ago.

Another fire festival is held in Valencia, Spain. Here enormous statues called *fallas*, which can take almost a year to build, are burned in the streets.

It is believed that this custom first started when local woodworkers had a spring clean and set fire to all their old wood chippings. Nowadays most of the town takes part in the celebrations.

Sixteenth century soccer

Twice a year an historic football match takes place in Florence, Italy. The game celebrates an heroic football match against invading troops that took place over four hundred years ago. All the players wear sixteenth century football kit.

Another strange football match takes place every year in Ashbourne, England. This match takes two days to complete and everyone in the town takes part. The two goals are 5 km (3 miles) apart and separated by a fast flowing stream. Eventually, most players end up soaking wet!

Celebrations in Belgium

In Belgium there are at least a thousand processions and festivals taking place throughout the year. One of the most famous is the Cat Procession at Ypres, where people dress up as cats and parade through the streets.

This custom celebrates the days when wood was stored in the Town Hall and cats were used to get rid of any rats and mice that made their nests in the timber.

See if you can find out about other celebrations in other countries.

If you have a penfriend (see page 9) ask them about traditions in their country.

NAME THE COUNTRIES

Look at the map of Europe. The names of the countries are written below but the letters have got muddled up. Unjumble the letters then write the correct country names in the spaces.
The first one has been done for you.

1 RED NAIL .... IRELAND ....

2 RAY WON ....

3 BUG MILE ....

4 GREY MAN ....

5 CER FAN ....

6 WAZ SID TRELN ....

7 RHAY GUN ....

8 IN SAP ....

9 GOAL SAY VIU ....

10 ME DRANK ....

11 DOT MINING DUKE ....

12 ED NEWS ....

13 LARD HEN NETS ....

14 PAL DON ....

15 AV COIL SOCK HAZE ....

16 AT RUSIA ....

17 GOAT PURL ....

18 LAY IT ....

19 REG EEC ....

20 MURE LUG BOX ....

Look at the map again. The letters A – P show the position of 16 European capitals. Match each letter to the correct capital city.

I've done one for you!

...O... Copenhagen   .... London
.... Paris   .... Stockholm
.... Vienna   .... Lisbon
.... Madrid   .... Bern
.... Oslo   .... Helsinki
.... Amsterdam   .... Athens
.... Rome   .... Brussels
.... Berlin   .... Warsaw

EUROQUIZ

1. How many countries are members of the European Community? ....
2. What is the capital of Germany? ....
3. What money is used in Greece? ....
4. What is the main language of the Netherlands? ....
5. Which country has the name 'España' on its stamps? ....
6. What famous tower was built for the Paris Exhibition of 1889? ....
7. Which country has the oldest national flag? ....
8. Lisbon is the capital of which country? ....
9. What is the highest mountain in the Alps? ....
10. Where would you see the Atomium? ....
11. Where are you most likely to spend pesetas? ....
12. What is the capital of Italy? ....
13. Where might you eat 'dolmades'? ......Greece......
14. Which country's flag is made up of three different flags? ....
15. What is the French word for 'Hello'? ......Bonjour......

Look back through the book to check your answers!

Ask an adult to mark them. See how many they get right.